MW01396411

Dedicated to

all Neurodiverse children and the allies who support them

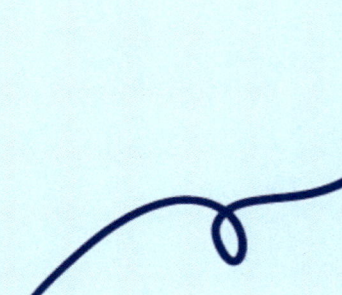

Copyright 202 Maxwell Palance, Heyon Choi

All rights reserved, The book, or parts thereof, may not be reproduced in any form without permission.

Produced in association with the Stanford Neurodiversity Project at Stanford University led by Dr. Lawrence Fung.

Published by Kindle Direct Publishing

Inquiries should be directed to: maxwellpalance@gmail.com

Font sourced from dafont.com
(Papernotes Regular)

My name is Max I'm just fifteen years old,

but I've got a unique story that needs to be told.

My life's been a journey to find my way.

Please come and join me, I have so much to say.

When I was young, I often cried
when riding on trains or going down slides.

I would get quite upset in a big, busy room,
and fall apart if I heard a loud noise or boom.

Transitions were so hard, I just didn't understand
why things were changing and not going as planned.

Wind and rain upset me. At parties, I was shy.
I didn't even like hugs, and I didn't know why.

My parents could see I was no typical boy.

At the beach, counting grains of sand brought ME joy.

Not a typical son, they were starting to see.

But they didn't yet know, I was Typically Me.

My parents did all that they could for me,

but they needed help, they had to agree.

An occupational therapist said things weren't so scary.

In time, it shouldn't be such a burden to carry.

So to speech and OT and play therapy I'd go,
and sometimes it seemed it was going sooo slow.

But, with practice, I found that I was calming down.

Little things that upset me stopped making me frown.

With repetition and early intervention,

in time, my challenges needed much less attention.

And, as I grew older, it all became clear,
I had ASD, which is nothing to fear.

Atypical is a word used to describe me.

Neurodiverse is another, you'll see.

But I wasn't sure that was who I might be.

I felt, in my heart, I was Typically Me.

In time, I discovered, to my surprise,

that ASD can be a gift in disguise.

For example, I found I was quite good at math

and learning coding put me on the right path.

Since autistic people love structure and routine,

they often have skills that go unseen.

With our great memories and attention to detail,

Our powers of focus allow us to prevail.

Some are great artists, visionaries, and musicians

or entrepreneurs in impressive positions.

In fact, I think it's important to mention

that Eintstein and Newton are both on the spectrum.

Many colleges know we enhance their community,
and Google and Microsoft seek out our ingenuity.

Some say I have a superpower, this ASD.

But I like to say, I'm just Typically Me.

I still don't like noises or beaches or flies,

or anything that might take me by surprise.

But I've learned to expect the unexpected,

and I do relaxation techniques till they're perfected.

Take a deep breath, close my eyes, count to three.

Kindly tell people to just let me be.

My mind may think something's a very big deal,

But with awareness, I can control how I feel.

You are meant to be the person you are.

Believing in that, you will surely go far.

Find your passion and use your unique gift for good.

Face your challenges and they will be understood.

We're all superheroes, and hour by hour,
we learn to develop our own superpowers.
The future is bright for us, as you can see.
I'm so proud to say that I'm TYPICALLY ME!

Acknowledgements

Stanford Neurodiversity Project (SNP)

SNP's Network for K-12 Neurodiversity Education and Advocacy (NNEA)

Dr. Lawrence Fung

About The Author and Illustrator

Diagnosed with Autism Spectrum Disorder as a toddler, Maxwel spent much of his childhood working with dedicated teachers and therapists to learn to navigate challenges and embrace the strengths of Neurodiversity. Today, Maxwell is a NASA N3 Intern and Scholar, accomplished mobile app developer, USA Computing Olympiad Platinum Level Computer Programmer, and Co-Chair of SNP's Network for K-12 Neurodiversity Education and Advocacy. After earning admission to Stanford Online High School, he now nourishes his love for math and computer science. He actively explores innovative ways to harness technology for meaningful impact and help others with conditions like his. Grateful for the support of the Stanford Neurodiversity Project, Maxwell writes to inspire every Neurodiverse child to discover the powerful possibilities within.

Heyon Choi is an illustrator and advocate for neurodiversity, dedicated to using art as a tool for social change. For nine years, Heyon has combined a passion for creativity with a commitment to helping others, leading initiatives such as founding Share & Spread, a non-profit that designs and sells merchandise to support various causes. An award-winning artist recognized in competitions like Scholastic Arts and the Genius Olympiad, Heyon has a deep commitment to promoting autistic artists. This involves curating exhibitions and creating impactful merchandise to showcase their talents and raise awareness. Heyon plans to continue this mission with a vision of fostering an inclusive society that celebrates diverse talents and perspectives.

Made in the USA
Monee, IL
24 September 2025